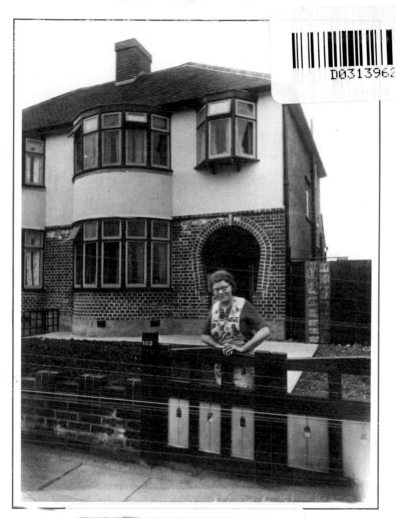

Lydia Watson standing proudly outside her new [...] Kidbrooke, in south-east London, in 1936. The [...] was still to be developed

TH[E 1930s] HOME

The Shire Book

For Alyssa Ruby

Published in 2000 by Shire Publications Ltd,
Cromwell House, Church Street, Princes Risborough,
Buckinghamshire HP27 9AA, UK.
(Website: www.shirebooks.co.uk)

British Library Cataloguing in Publication Data:
Stevenson, Greg
The 1930s home. – (The Shire book)
1. Architecture, Domestic – Great Britain – History –
20th century
2. Interior decoration – Great Britain – History – 20th
century
I. Title II. The nineteen-thirties home
728'0941'09043
ISBN 0 7478 0464 8

Front cover: *An original brochure for Wates builders. Purchasers could choose their favourite house style and have it built for them on one of a number of estates.*

Back cover: *'Stillness', a house designed by the architect Gilbert Booth in 1934.*

ACKNOWLEDGEMENTS
The author is very grateful to all those who supplied photographs or allowed him to photo-
graph their homes. Thanks go to Alan Aspden, Paul Barnfather, Martin Black, Sally
Edwards, Tim Elmhirst, Richard Feachem, Bryan Fry, Rachel and Garry Freeman, Zoë
Hendon, Clive Hooley, Sylvia Katz, Dr R. Pletts, Joan Rayner, Quentin Rubens, Jill Theis,
June Victor, Quentin Willson and the residents of Llys Meirion in Caernarfon. Photographs
are reproduced with the kind permission of: Alan Aspden, page 12 (top); Martin Black
Photography, pages 8 (top), 20 (top), 21 (centre), 40 and back cover; Carmarthenshire
County Museum, page 28 (bottom left); Ceredigion Museum, page 33 (bottom); Croydon
Museum and Heritage Service, pages 4, 5 (all four), 6 (bottom), 7 (top), 9 (top left and top
right), 10, 11 (bottom), 12 (centre), 14 (top), 17 (bottom), 22 (all three), 23 (all three), 24
(top), 25 (centre), 30 (top), 31 (bottom), 35 (bottom), 36 (bottom), 38 (both); the De La
Warr Pavilion Trust, page 8 (bottom); the Geffrye Museum, pages 13 (bottom), 21 (bottom); the Gnome Reserve, page 36 (top); the Katz Collection, page 32 (top and bottom
left); the Museum of Domestic Design and Architecture, Middlesex University, pages 24
(centre two), 25 (top right); the Museum of Welsh Life, St Fagans, pages 6 (top), 18 (centre
and bottom); Plastics Historical Society, page 33 (top). Special thanks go to my parents for
scanning the images.

Printed in Wales by CIT Printing Services Ltd, Press
Buildings, Merlins Bridge, Haverfordwest,
Pembrokeshire SA61 1XF.

CONTENTS

Bedroom designed for William Whiteley Ltd, London, and pictured in 'Studio' magazine in 1936. The wooden 'Plan' furniture was designed by Serge Chermayeff and the curtain fabric described as 'absolutely fadeless and resistant to sea air'.

INTRODUCTION

More dream homes were constructed in the 1930s than have been built in any decade since. Many people became home-owners for the first time during the inter-war period and the four million houses that were erected for them largely adopted new architectural styles. These styles varied from sleek modernist villas to 'Tudorbethan' semi-detached houses, with many blends of traditional and modern styles in between. Not only were these new homes different in that they were designed to meet the demands of the changing family, but they could also provide a variety of fantasy interiors and revolutionary technologies for their new owners. Many young couples moving into their newly built homes in the 1930s really were experiencing a new way of living, with all-electric kitchens, plumbed-in bathrooms and often a garden of their own.

The new houses of the 1930s reflected the improving living standards and increased income of the majority of the population. Although remote rural areas remained virtually untouched by the new architecture and many people continued to live in poverty, real incomes were improving for most. The increased availability of affordable mortgages and a variety of hire-purchase schemes for everything from furnishings to cars meant that many were able to own and furnish their own home for the first time. People who had previously rented houses in urban Victorian terraces moved out to semi-detached suburban homes, which could be bought for between £400 and £1500, depending on their facilities and proximity to London. New housing styles were often seen on these estates, as well as in municipal homes, apartments and the luxury villas of the rich.

'Each house individual!'. A middle-class family selects their dream home, as built by Wates builders in 1939.

With a wireless in almost every home, and twenty million people visiting the cinema every week, people became aware of the latest domestic fashions through advertisements and films. The average householder became increasingly fashion-conscious and the cult of

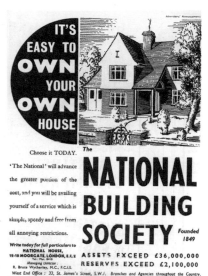

Above left: *Kitchen design improved dramatically now that hired help was becoming scarce. The text for this publicity photograph boasts of 'hot and cold water at the turn of a tap'.*

Above right: *The increased availability of afford-able mortgages enabled more people than ever before to purchase their own home.*

Left: *'Coulsdon Heights. Your Home in the Country – Close to Town'. Sales brochures sold an image of the country idyll.*

Below: *By 1939 three out of every four households had a radio. Through radio, cinema and magazine advertisements people became aware of the latest domestic styles.*

Rural areas remote from the south-east of England retained their traditional way of life, architecture and furnishings. Here quilt wives display their work at Solva, Pembrokeshire, in 1929.

home décor developed alongside booming sales of magazines such as *Good Housekeeping* and *Modern Home*. The *Daily Express* proclaimed in its popular book *The Home of Today* that 'Men and women are equally enthusiastic – a new consciousness of home-making has been born!'

The 1930s home was typically designed to suit the modern family, which had changed significantly since Victorian times. By 1930 the previously rapid population growth appeared to be levelling out, families were on average considerably smaller, and many middle-class families had only two children. Domestic service had disappeared in all but the homes of the very rich. New houses therefore had to be manageable for those who maintained them.

The typical suburban 1930s home consisted of a front lounge, dining room, a small kitchen (from which mother could keep an eye on the children in the back garden), three bedrooms (one being a box room for a baby) and a small bathroom. Many semi-detached homes were built for newlywed couples, with several developers giving them appropriate 'starter-home' names, such as Honeymoon Cottage. It is interesting to note that the formal reception room (the 'front

The new homes were built to accommodate the modern family, which often included only two children. The text for this publicity photograph reads: 'Everything planned for your comfort – down to the aerial and earth for your radio'.

The master bedroom in semi-detached homes was typically furnished as a luxury room for the lady of the house. This particular arrangement was advertised as 'aiding restful sleep'.

room') survived as a showpiece although in practice it was used perhaps only one day in any week, as keeping two coal fires alight would have been too expensive. The back reception room (sold as a dining room) often became the centre of family life. By contrast, in modern flats and expensive private villas there was a progression towards open-plan interiors and retractable partitions in rooms heated by electric fires or under-floor heating.

Most newly built houses were of two-storey construction and were built on green-belt land on the edge of towns. Greatly improved public transport, an increase in the ownership of cars, and the relative affordability of land outside the urban core resulted in a massive suburban expansion of detached and semi-detached homes, each having a small garden. Private housing was distinct from local authority terraced accommodation as each home or pair of homes was set within its own plot. Although

Park Royal station in west London, on the Piccadilly Line of the Underground, was designed by the architects Charles Holden and S. A. Heaps whilst Frank Pick was the design director. Improved public transport in Greater London facilitated expansion to the suburbs.

most 1930s homes were smaller than those constructed before the First World War, they were generally built on a larger piece of land. The suburban growth was particularly evident around London: between 1921 and 1937 the population of Inner London declined by half a million while the area of Greater London swelled by a million and a quarter.

Typical advertisements from the speculative builders who built these new suburban estates proclaimed the benefits of 'living in the country where you will have room to breathe'. The theme of light, clean family homes was common in advertisements for houses as diverse as cottage-style bungalows and modernist apartments. This escape from the polluted city to the healthy suburban fringe was epitomised in the styling of semi-detached homes, which borrowed old-fashioned 'historical' architectural features and typically made obvious reference to the rural cottage idyll. New suburban estates were often supplemented with small shopping centres and public utilities, ranging from post-offices to church halls, libraries to cinemas, all frequently built in matching architectural styles. For many the move to a new home in suburbia brought a new way of life.

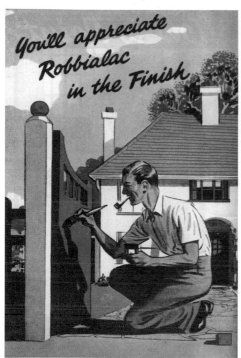

Above: *Department stores in town centres provided customers with everything they needed for their new homes. Bowmans of Camden Town, London, specialised in Modern Movement interiors.*

Left: *An advertisement for Robbialac paint. With more and more people owning their own homes, maintaining a tidy house frontage became increasingly important.*

The 'Oxford Group' as supplied by Drages department store. £22 10s would have purchased all the furniture shown, and customers could pay in fifty monthly instalments.

ARCHITECTURAL STYLES

The architectural styles of 1930s homes were many and varied. On the one hand flat-roofed villas were being built by architects influenced by continental Modernism, and on the other pseudo-historical-styled semi-detached houses were being built by speculative builders. In between these extremes of modern and traditional were many houses which borrowed elements of both architectural styles. People were not afraid to create a pastiche of new and old, of continental and British styles. In any one street houses as different as a jettied mock-Tudor dormer bungalow and an uncompromisingly functionalist Internationalist-style home could be built. Original sales brochures reveal that the individual nature of each house was part of the appeal.

For many the 1930s home presented the opportunity of having the best of both worlds – the country cottage with 'all mod cons' within easy reach of the city. A new home often represented the fulfilment of a long-held aspiration to own a timber-clad home or a light, modern flat. It is perhaps for this reason that we see such wonderful variety and so many fantasy designs in the homes of the era.

Local authorities erected many estates of short terraces of houses, as well as blocks of flats. These invariably continued the tradition of neo-Georgian properties popularised by Louis de Soissons at Welwyn Garden City. The neo-Georgian style was used so often in local authority housing that it became a symbol of the council-owned home. Often the estates were large, 120,000 people being housed in one such estate alone at Becontree near Dagenham, Essex. Unfortunately the builders of owner-occupied developments usually ignored the good planning and effective layout of these local authority estates.

Most of the new privately owned homes built between 1930 and 1940 were three-bedroom semi-detached homes in pseudo-historical styles on suburban estates. But whereas council housing was characterised by its architectural uniformity, there was a conscious attempt with privately owned houses to celebrate their individuality with bay windows, scallop-edged leadwork, leaded-glass windows and half-timbering.

The 'individual' designs of private housing were part of the sales pitch included in builders' brochures.

Above left: *Local authority housing typically adopted the neo-Georgian style made popular by the garden-city movement and had double hung 'Georgian' sash windows. This late example is one of the less common types that had modern-styled fittings.*

Above right: *A typical semi-detached home in a Cardiff suburb. Note the mature tree in the foreground, deliberately planted to add a rural feel to the estate.*

Tile-hung gables, nogged brick or herringbone-pattern panels, as well as unnecessarily ornate chimneys, appeared on new houses across Britain. Often huge gables dropped down over bay windows almost to the ground, conveniently incorporating a porch. This, and some of the other features (leaded lights, rustic lanterns, half-timbering), had much in common with the architecture of the later Arts and Crafts movement and the work of the architect C. F. A. Voysey.

The semi-detached houses of suburbia fostered an individualism bordering on snobbery. Many people owned their own homes for the first time and were keen to maintain the 'tone' and the property prices of their area. Public displays of being well-to-do thus became more important than ever. The wider plot width allowed for the inclusion of a tradesman's entrance from the garden, thus giving a privacy that many residents had probably not previously enjoyed. From the white picket fence to the vase in the bay window, a show of good taste became significant in people's

THE UNIVERSAL HOUSE at the IDEAL HOME EXHIBITION EARLS COURT 1939

For the princely sum of £2250 purchasers could own the fantasy 'Universal' house with stepped Dutch gables and romantic balconies.

'Haystacks' in south Oxfordshire was brick-built in 1934 to an octagonal plan with 'Gothick' casement windows and a thatched roof.

A top-of-the-range exhibition house of 1939 displays French casement windows and is finished in cream and ivory paintwork.

Below: With a built-in garage and jettied first floor, this detached house on a Surrey estate mixed the modern and traditional.

lives. Owners of semi-detached houses in suburbia looked down on neo-Georgian council estates and, in a few instances, even built high walls to keep their poorer neighbours out of sight. However, it was often their own homes that were the examples of poor design and wasteful use of land.

A semi generally cost about £100 less than a detached house. They were so popular that a few were sold for as much as £2500 (more than the cost of a large detached house). Detached homes were sometimes built to the plans of a semi and so appear as if they have lost their other half. In a few cases small blocks of four flats and even terraced homes were designed to appear from the exterior to be semi-detached.

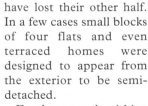

For those people wishing to remain in inner suburbs or city centres, some modern flats were built. Many of these were rented out in the first instance, and for annual payments

Above: *Nugents Court at Hatch End in Middlesex had bay windows on the second floor. The stepped decorative rendering over the entrance nods to contemporary Art Deco fashions.*

Above: *Pinner Court at Pinner in Middlesex typifies the British Moderne style with its curved 'Sun-Trap' windows and Hollywood balconies.*

Left: *Colebrook Close in Putney, southwest London, was built in 1936 for renting to starlets from a film studio. For £195 per annum residents enjoyed central heating, two bathrooms and a built-in jewel safe for their diamonds!*

ranging from £70 to £150 tenants could enjoy central heating and the services of a porter. Some of these buildings echoed the half-timbered mock-Tudor style of suburbia, but the majority adopted restrained, modern decoration.

A period room-setting of a 1930s flat on display at the Geffrye Museum, London.

13

'All the advantages of a private house with the convenience of a modern flat'. The 'Rochester' bungalow was available to buy for 22s 9d per week 'all-in' in 1939.

Bungalows were a particularly favoured form of housing in the inter-war years, and in some areas whole estates of bungalows, both semi-detached and detached, were built. People could see single-storey homes on the silver screen and wanted the same 'Hollywood' style for themselves. As with houses on more than one storey, a variety of architectural styles was evident.

Despite its popularity on the continent the Modern Movement style was little favoured in Britain. Few dared risk building an estate of flat-roofed houses, with their expanses of metal-framed windows and innovative concrete technology. Those that were built were constructed largely by traditional means and decorated to appear in the Modern Movement style. In 1934 you could buy a three-bedroom flat-roofed semi in West Molesey, Surrey, for just £395. The brochure declares: 'This flat roof offers you a whole floor of extra space ... your children can play in safety and in unrestricted sunshine ... enjoy the peace of moonlight and sleep *al fresco* if you wish.'

Whereas it is unlikely that many of these home-owners did sleep

A Modern-styled villa designed by Ernest Freud for Mrs D. Cottington Taylor, director of the Good Housekeeping Institute, in 1937. Note the glazed wall and flat roof, typical of the era.

White Wings, Paignton, Devon, designed by the architect William Lescase and built by Staverton in 1935. The similarity to continental Modern Movement villas is explained by the fact that Lescase was taught by Swiss architect Le Corbusier.

Left: *British Modern Movement architecture at its best. The third Sun House at Amersham, Buckinghamshire, viewed from the rear gardens. One of a group of four completed in 1934 by the architects Connell, Ward and Lucas.*

Below: *High and Over, Amersham, Buckinghamshire. View of the north-west wing from the south terrace. Completed 1929–30 by Connell, Ward and Lucas. Unlike many of the houses that emulated the work of these architects, High and Over was of truly modern construction.*

under the stars, the large windows and balconies on such homes must have brought a bright freshness into the lives of those who dared 'go modern'. A year after their launch the houses at West Molesey were being sold with added pitched roofs: for many purchasers a flat roof had proved just too different. In some cases building societies were cautious about giving mortgages on the white-walled flat-roofed villas, fearing difficulty in resale. The modern style was the accepted form for factories and the workplace, but most people wanted to come home to a cottagey retreat at the end of the day.

A large number of pseudo-modern (properly referred to as Moderne) homes were built, and in many cases the only difference between these and their 'Tudorbethan' neighbours was the use of simple metal-framed windows rather than wooden-framed bays with leaded lights. The so-called 'Sun-Trap' metal-framed windows with

Above left: *Flat-roofed homes were common in popular seaside resorts of the period, such as this example designed by Ronald H. Franks at Borth, Ceredigion. Because of the salty sea air this house has had some replacement windows and the first-floor bay originally had an open loggia, since glazed over.*

Above right: *This Moderne-styled semi was built in 1939 at Caernarfon, North Wales, by the builders Williams of Abersoch. 'Sun-Trap' metal-framed windows make the most of views across the Menai Straits.*

Below: *A Moderne-styled semi at Salt Hill in Slough, Berkshire. Note how half of the front elevation is rendered and half left in red brick. This example really does mix modern and traditional.*

curved corner glass made by Crittall's of Braintree, Essex, were particularly popular on Moderne homes. Occasionally these houses had green or blue glazed pantiles on their pitched roofs, to be like the houses seen in Hollywood, and sun-ray motifs on fixtures such as the garden gate.

It is interesting to note that, whether bungalow or semi, country-cottage or Moderne, the majority of these homes were built by speculative builders with little input from architects. Often the money made from selling homes at one end of the street would help to build the houses at the other end. Larger firms employed architects to prepare series of designs that they could repeat on different estates. Those that did employ an architect were likely to advertise the fact in their sales literature.

The few privately commissioned Modern villas that were architect-designed were often innovative in their structure and their style. Relatively new materials such as reinforced concrete allowed architects to design homes with huge areas of glazed wall and balconies that appear to hang without support. The work of architects such as Colin Lucas, Maxwell Fry, Serge Chermayeff and Gilbert Booth was progressive but exceptional. The majority conformed to the style of the 'Tudorbethan' semi.

The 'Lyndhurst' bedroom suite was available at Drages department stores in Birmingham and London for £23 10s. Customers could pay in fifty monthly instalments.

FURNISHINGS

A 1933 vase in the 'Coral Firs' pattern designed by Clarice Cliff. Moderne ceramics had traditional images painted in bright colours on modern shapes.

Although some people brought their old furniture into their new 1930s homes, a surprisingly large number invested in new home furnishings. Many people moving out of rented furnished accommodation had to buy whole sets of furniture, and department stores provided hire-purchase schemes to enable them to do just that. Hamptons furnishers, for example, would provide all the furnishings (including carpets and curtains) for a six-roomed house for £235, including carriage to any railway station within Great Britain.

There had been department stores before the First World War but their numbers increased greatly during the inter-war years. They provided the perfect shopping ground for the new suburbans – a single shop from which people could get everything they needed for their complete home style. Stores provided sample room-settings in different styles and customers could walk from department to department selecting the furniture, soft furnishings and decorative goods to provide the look that they desired. There was a large choice of styles, from restrained classical, French decorative or English oak to tubular-steel modern, and everything from tables to tea-sets to complement that image. Affordable versions of old oak furniture or streamlined modern styles were readily available for every room in the home.

For those who preferred to make their own furniture, magazines such as *The Hobbyist* provided detailed instructions and pull-out plans to construct 'Jacobean' cupboards. Throughout the inter-war years more workers

17

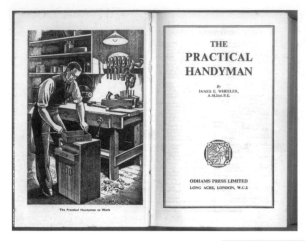

Many people made their own furniture, encouraged by books such as 'The Practical Handyman' and magazines such as 'Hobbyist'.

Quakers set up a co-operative furniture factory to aid the depressed South Wales town of Brynmawr. This 1939 photograph shows workers constructing chairs designed by Paul Matt.

A London showroom displays the finished products from Brynmawr. Philanthropic purchasers could buy the best Arts and Crafts tradition furniture in the modern style and feel they were supporting the working classes.

than ever before enjoyed a two-day weekend and an increasing number of people had time to spend on DIY projects. Housekeeping books provided practical suggestions on how to up-date Victorian furniture with paint and panel-boarding.

The dining room in the house of Hayes Marshall, the head of Fortnum & Mason's decorating department, pictured in 'Studio' magazine, November 1936. Note the plaster fan-shaped bowl fixed to the wall and the horse's head by the French potter Colet Gueden.

Left: *Traditional chair shapes dating from the nineteenth century remained in mass production throughout the 1930s.*

Below: *Romantic bedroom interiors little changed from the 1920s and earlier were popular throughout the decade.*

The furniture of the 1930s home was generally smaller than that designed for the large high-ceilinged rooms of Victorian and Edwardian properties. That said, the popular oak sideboards of the period were often built in massive proportions. Much of the furniture was constructed out of cheap softwoods and plywood because of a shortage of good timber that continued from the 1920s. To compensate for this, many pieces were veneered in oak or exotic fruitwoods. Built-in furniture, particularly for the bedroom and the kitchen, became more popular and, although many associate fitted kitchen units with the 1950s, they were in vogue in the 1930s.

The furnishings of the 1930s

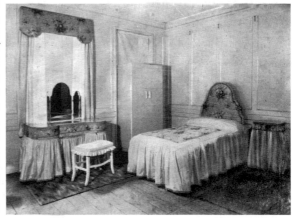

home generally follow two quite different styles: a pastiche of the styles of the Tudor, Jacobean or Georgian periods, and the 'Streamline Moderne' or 'Jazz-Modern' style. Very often there would be a combination of these incongruous fashions, and a dining table that harked back to a romantic vision of the past would stand next to a futuristic 'machine-age' radio cabinet. Occasionally even individual pieces of furniture blended the two styles. For example, sofas were produced with sharply geometric forms but 'country cottage' floral upholstery. Others had traditional chesterfield shapes yet were upholstered in fabrics with cubist-inspired designs. Oak-veneer furniture occasionally blended modernistic outlines with cabriole or barley-twist legs. Many people who purchased the new square-armed three-piece suites still covered them with crocheted antimacassars.

The new furniture types of the era, such as radio cabinets, speaker boxes and cocktail cabinets, were usually in the modern style and

Left: For those who preferred the contemporary style, modern bedroom furnishings in the French Art Deco style were available.

Cocktail cabinets often took on fanciful shapes, such as this example in an exotic wood veneer. Note the Murphy radio to the right.

decorated with fretwork panels depicting stylised images of the sun rising. Even the most traditional interiors with restrained old-fashioned styles of furnishings were likely to have a modern radio by the late 1930s. The next most popular concession to the modern style was one of the new boxy lounge suites. The chairs of these were considerably bulkier than their 1920s counterparts and copied the Hollywood styles with their simple geometric outlines and bulbous forms familiar from the cinemas.

The Jacobean-inspired oak furniture was as different from the original as the 'Jazz-Modern' pieces were from the continental Modernist designs they mimicked. Poorly proportioned oak cabinets, tables and sideboards haphazardly blended

Above: *Period furnishings and an original carpet in remarkable condition in a restored semi at Croxley Green on the Metropolitan line in Hertfordshire.*

Left: *A continental Art Deco dining suite and other period furnishings in a restored dining room. Note the provision of two doors. The wealthy owner could still afford domestic help and one door was reserved for 'staff'.*

Typical suburban lounge, formerly on display at the Geffrye Museum, London. Note the heavy oak sideboard and crocheted antimacassars.

21

A popular design for a bedroom suite, this set cost 29 guineas in 1935. Note the eiderdown quilt on the bed.

'You can always rely on the Finns to design something attractive and original' reads the advertisement for this dining suite by Alvar Aalto. Now regarded as a classic of twentieth-century design, the tea wagon (to the right) cost just £4 15s in 1935.

decorative styles from the fifteenth to the seventeenth centuries. The 1932 book *Suggestions for Modern Furnishing* attacked such design:

> As a counsel of despair a jerry-built 'Tudor' villa is best furnished with cheap 'Jacobean' oak, for the one is counterpart to the other: but it is painful to reflect that such hideous developments are a product of modern civilization and were unknown even amidst the 'ignorance and superstition' of medievalism.

A boxy lounge suite is complemented by a bowl vase designed by Keith Murray, an enviable ceramic accessory of the period.

Above left: *Space-saving furniture in a 'Bachelor's Modern Flat' setting at Bowmans department store in Camden Town, London, in 1935. Note the telephone by the day-bed.*

Above right: *Flexible furniture arrangements were popular during the 1930s. Minty provided bookcases to fit any space in 'Standard', 'Modern' or 'Neo-craft' finishes in 1935.*

Furniture in the Moderne style was generally angular in shape with stepped and symmetrical outlines, and wrap-around veneer surfaces. Very often it incorporated the new plastic Bakelite (itself indicative of the 'bright, new age') in handles and fittings. Other modern-style pieces were produced in steam-bent plywood copying the work of the Finnish designer and architect Alvar Aalto or in tubular steel by the British company PEL (Practical Equipment Ltd). Chromed-steel tubular chairs and tables were particularly popular, and Bauhaus-inspired pieces by Marcel Breuer and Mies van der Rohe were produced by Thonet and available on the high street. Such modern furnishings were appropriate for flat-roofed villas and high-rise flats, but often the odd piece would creep into the old-world charm of the 'Tudorbethan' semi. The owners of a 1930s home could happily combine styles from four centuries of design and still be 'with the times'.

On the floors were a variety of carpet squares and linoleum coverings or, in more expensive homes, a parquet oak floor (to match oak-panelled walls) in the hallway and possibly reception rooms. The pine floorboards in the bedrooms were often varnished in a dark 'Jacobean' stained varnish or fitted with linoleum sporting either traditional

The carpet hall of Bowmans department store in 1935. The 'Seamless Axminster' to the rear cost £6 11s 3d, and the 'Twentieth Century Carpet' to the foreground was an expensive £17 5s.

23

Exhibited at the Royal Academy exhibition in 1935, this circular rug by Margaret Blondel could be made in any colour and cost £22 5s.

Two 1934 designs for rugs by John Churton for the Silver Studio, now housed in the Museum of Domestic Design and Architecture, Middlesex University.

Left: *Wallpapers such as this example were popular in shades of brown, orange and red (known as 'autumn tints') throughout the 1930s and, though they were despised by writers on design, their popularity continued until the 1950s.*

floral or modern geometric motifs. Bathrooms had either red tiled floors or linoleum in abstract patterns and the kitchens had quarry tiles or linoleum. Rugs often had cubist-inspired geometric patterning.

Walls were painted or wallpapered with co-ordinating borders and corners. There was even a wallpaper in antique wood effect. Anaglypta papers imitating Jacobean plaster ceilings were popular as were many floral patterns for bedrooms. As with carpets and soft furnishings, the most popular colours for wallpapers were autumnal browns, oranges and reds, known at the time as 'autumn tints'. Modern homes featured plain monochrome walls with decorative borders and corner

Far left: *Original linoleum in a 'Jazz-Modern' pattern.*

Left: *Linoleum was a popular floor covering in bedrooms, bathrooms and kitchens.*

Left: *Popular modern curtain fabrics as advertised in 1935 at prices of between 3 and 15 shillings a yard.*

Right: *A 1930 advertisement from 'Modern Home' magazine illustrates a chintzy floral upholstery fabric and ceramic bowls by Clarice Cliff.*

pieces, and often stepped plywood pelmets over the windows. New soft-furnishing fabrics such as Rayon led to a range of new textures in curtain fabrics. There was still a market for traditional cloth, however, and in 1933 the Welsh Textiles Association was established to produce upholstery fabrics and tweeds for sale in London. Perhaps metropolitan consumers felt they were helping depressed rural areas in which the new-age furnishings and houses were largely unknown.

FIXTURES AND FITTINGS

Above: *This 1939 semi in North Wales has a Georgian revival door and 'Sun-Trap' metal-framed windows under a decorative Regency-style pelmet. Only the British Moderne style could mix such influences!*

The fixtures and fittings installed in 1930s homes were usually designed to complement the architectural style of the property, be it traditional or modern. Cast-iron door furniture that had changed little in style since 1900 was still fitted on traditional homes, yet modern-styled houses were more likely to have angular chromed latches and handles that reflected contemporary fashions.

Windows were usually double hung sash in local authority housing (emulating Georgian examples) but almost exclusively wood or metal casement in owner-occupied houses. Closely associated with the semi-detached home is the bay window, which allowed home-owners to view both up and down the street as well as the houses across the road. Windows to the front and sides of properties were often fitted with leaded glass lights, continuing the Arts and Crafts tradition of using lead to create decorative patterns. Common images were

'Sun-Trap' metal-framed bay windows were made by Crittall's of Braintree in Essex. Unfortunately many lost their curved glass corners when plastic-framed replacement windows became popular in the 1990s.

Above left: *Coloured-glass lights with decorative leadwork remained popular in windows from the beginning of the twentieth century through to the Second World War. Many suburban semi-detached homes had decorative window lights such as this one.*

Above right: *This quintessentially 1930s door was designed in 1937 by the architect Griffith Morris of Porthmadog for a house in Aberystwyth, Ceredigion. The glass was supplied by Pilkingtons.*

stylised flowers, the sun rising, galleons and country cottages. Some new leaded window lights were made with contrived 'repairs' to try and add a feeling of authenticity to pseudo-historical properties. The pseudo-modern Moderne homes also adopted coloured-glass leaded-light windows, and these often featured chevrons and stylised sun-ray patterns. Truly Modern houses would not have had such fussy decorative features.

Fireplaces on the ground floor of most new homes of the 1930s were still for coal and were typically fitted with either a modern tile or traditional oak surround. Bedrooms were more often installed with electric fires, and in some houses these flush-fitting appliances were provided throughout. In Modern Movement homes daring architects might not have included any fireplaces as they would have planned for underfloor heating.

Although black-leaded coal ranges

Below: *Modern homes and flats might have had a modern chrome fireplace such as this 1935 example.*

Left: *This cast-iron Allustre fire-place (£3 19s 10d in 1936) has been enamelled to give it a modern look.*

Below: *Farmhouse kitchen featured in 'Studio' magazine, 1936. Note the ventilated cupboards under the window and the Aga, which was guaranteed to cost no more than £5 a year to run.*

Left: *A scullery kitchen reconstructed at Carmarthenshire County Museum, showing the cramped conditions of many kitchens of the period.*

remained in common use before the First World War, many new homes of the 1930s had one of the new closed-in enamelled ranges (the Aga dating from 1929), or a gas or electric cooker. These appliances were often supplemented with an enamelled coke boiler to heat the kitchen and the hot water. Linoleum, which was used for floors in place of quarry tiles, was also used on tabletops for ease of cleaning. Much thought was given to the way kitchens were laid out so that there was minimal walking distance between preparation, cooking and washing areas. As refrigerators were an expensive luxury, a larder was usually provided, north-facing and with a gauze window to keep the food cool. Crockery was stored on a rack or in a free-standing kitchen cupboard.

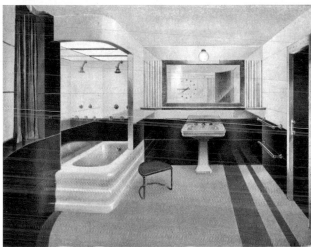

Above left: *Featured in 'Good Housekeeping' magazine in 1937, this kitchen 'is planned to save steps and avoid expenditure of needless energy'.*

Above right: *Low-level toilet cisterns became popular in the 1930s; pipes and accessories were often chromed.*

Left: *'A Modern Bathroom by Harrods' in the 'Streamline Moderne' style, reflecting contemporary concerns about hygiene.*

Bathrooms and kitchens became the domain of the polished surface and tiled wall and were typically finished with polished chrome fittings. They were often designed with the contemporary concerns of hygiene and efficiency in mind and house brochures boasted about 'non-dust-collecting cornices' and walls 'tiled to dado height'. For many people, having a plumbed-in bath and a toilet indoors was a new luxury, and it is not surprising that bathrooms were often in the modern style. A large expanse of wall-tiling was a desirable feature: the higher the tiles reached up a wall, the greater the social standing of the owner.

TECHNOLOGY IN THE HOME

Newly built houses of the 1930s were fitted with electric lighting and power points. Although a few local authority 'all-gas' flats were still being built in 1930, electricity had become standard for lighting. Homes in urban areas were often also supplied with gas for the cooker and copper water cylinder.

For many people moving into a house which had electric lighting and sockets, a plumbed-in internal bathroom and toilet, and hot water on tap, it was a move into the modern world. The annual *Daily Mail* Ideal Home exhibition was a popular event which aimed to educate these new home-owners in consumerism. As domestic service went into decline such shows featured the labour-saving devices that housewives could buy with hire-purchase schemes. Some new appliances, such as electric toasters, were proudly displayed within the home while others, such as vacuum cleaners, were kept out of sight if owners preferred to hide the fact that they no longer hired domestic help.

Above: *'Hot water without restriction', boasts a 1939 house brochure for Wates builders.*

The battle between gas and electricity suppliers for customers continued well into the decade. Gas-powered refrigerators, dish-washers and washing machines were all available, though at a high price. The popular cookery writer Elizabeth Craig was paid by the Electrical Development Association in 1937 to condone the use of electricity in the home:

> If you want to reduce the work in your kitchen to a minimum, electrify your kitchen. If you're a business woman, you simply can't do without one, in these days when time is money. An all-electric kitchen is no longer a luxury – it is a necessity.

A feast fit for a king? An Esse solid-fuel cooker advertisement uses the 1937 coronation to improve sales.

ISSUED BY THE BRITISH COMMERCIAL GAS ASSOCIATION
1, Grosvenor Place, London, S.W.

Advertised Goods are Good Goods. 165

Far left: *'Achieved in the Service of the Home', a 1937 advertisement for the Parkinson gas cooker. Note the Moderne house pictured top left.*

Left: *A gas refrigerator was available for 2s 6d a week in 1937, yet most homes made do with the cool larder. Interestingly, the silent, efficient gas-powered refrigerator would later be superseded by electric models that were less efficient.*

Brighter light bulbs meant that improved shading was needed (previously bulbs had often been left bare), and a variety of glass and plastic shades were produced in traditional and modern styles. Particularly popular were round hanging bowl shades and wall brackets. Modern-styled homes sometimes had strip lights, newly invented, concealed in niches and furniture to provide a diffused glow.

'Keeping up with the times' was a driving force behind the acquisition of many of the new domestic goods. 'Efficiency' and 'freedom' were the advertising buzzwords of the day, and science was heralded as the saviour of the housewife and a key to an effortless domestic future. The reality was that many electric appliances were expensive and inefficient and their use was not as widespread as the volume of advertising might suggest. There were many inconsistencies in electricity supply, and different suburbs of some towns used different AC and DC systems. A move for the householder could thus have proved expensive if their devices

Gas and flat irons – the modern and traditional, both in regular use in the 1930s home.

31

A 1930s room-setting from the American publication 'Modern Plastics' which illustrates the use of new plastics in the home for flooring, wall panels, doors, cups and cigarette boxes.

Below left: *A Bakelite lamp holder in the stepped Art Deco style.*

Below right: *Telephones were becoming widespread by the end of the 1930s. This oak telephone table was highly recommended at the Royal Institute of British Architects Exhibition of Everyday Things in 1936.*

Bakelite domestic goods. The new plastics of the period introduced stream-lined shapes into the home.

were rendered useless. For this reason the most popular appliances were the smaller and cheaper ones, such as electric irons. In 1935 only 25 per cent of households had an electric iron, yet this had risen to 75 per cent by the outbreak of the Second World War four years later. The kitchen was home to several small electrical appliances such as kettles, toasters, waffle irons and plate warmers. Some of these were given names that referred directly to them as wageless servants, such as the Atmos 'Housemaid', which could wash dishes and wash, press and iron clothes as well as vacuum-clean.

By the mid 1930s almost every home was using a radio receiver, and its effect in bringing the wider world into the British home should not be underestimated. For the first time the entire British nation became aware of the latest events, stories and fashions. Television was soon to follow for those in the London area who could afford the expensive sets. These newly developed appliances not only changed life and leisure within the home, but also brought the world to one's doorstep.

An electric Ekco radio in the classic round Bakelite case of the period. This example was made in 1945 and is on display at Ceredigion Museum.

THE GARDEN

Many of the inhabitants of the newly built homes of the period were enjoying their own garden for the first time. Not only were people moving out to 'the country' on suburban estates, they also wanted their own piece of countryside, and the garden was a key element of the rural idyll depicted in advertising brochures. In reality most houses were provided with a small, square patch of land that was not even seeded for lawn.

The garden of the 1930s home was an important leisure area and gardening was a popular activity often supported by local clubs and competitions. With a reduction in working office hours, many people found they had time to relax in their garden. The small squares of land allocated in each plot became intensively developed with rockeries, ponds, gnome gardens, crazy-paved seating areas, and structures such as glasshouses or sheds.

Front gardens were generally reserved for formal display and typically consisted of a small patch of lawn surrounded by tidy

Left: *A low front wall and formal display beds were popular on suburban estates of semi-detached homes.*

The front garden of this 1939 house in Newcastle Emlyn, Ceredigion, displays a typical combination of lawn and formal borders.

flower borders, enclosed by a brick wall low enough for passers-by to see over. Flowering shrubs such as tea roses and summer bedding plants such as begonias, lobelias and alyssums were all popular. The grass verges that often ran alongside the roads on newly built estates added to the rural aspect. Simply laying a lawn and flower borders was itself a social statement, as the poor had to use any land they had as a kitchen garden. The historical fantasy represented by mock-Tudor styling on the fronts of houses was complemented by 'magical' rockery gardens for the fairies and elves. Gnomes, which date from the 1880s, were common on suburban estates, as were concrete wishing-wells and other fantasy features.

The typical rear garden of the average suburban semi was an oblong patch of land measuring about 9 metres by 24 metres (30 feet by 80 feet). This space was very different

Above: *A sun canopy was a desirable garden accessory on the rear patio of houses.*

Left: *The rear garden was an important leisure area for the family, and several companies specialised in providing garden furniture and accessories.*

Home sweet home. Earthenware gnomes such as this 1930 example were a popular addition to fantasy rockery scenes in front gardens of suburban semi-detached homes.

from the front lawn, being a private area screened by high weather-boarding fences. It was generally split between a patio area nearest to the house (often crazy-paved and occasionally having a sun canopy), a lawn where the children could play and decorative borders to the middle section, and a vegetable garden sited at the far end. Small glasshouses were also occasionally sited at the bottom of the garden, behind a privet hedge, as was the garden shed. By the end of the decade many suburbans were building air-raid shelters at the end of their gardens, often completely below ground level, with a substantial rockery above. All manner of accessories were popular – birdbaths (sometimes in twee thatched-cottage styles), concrete statues, sundials and rustic benches. The garden had become 'styled' in the same way that the front room was furnished with fashionable consumables.

The garden shed at the bottom of the garden could sometimes be a more substantial work-shop, such as this example behind a Cardiff semi.

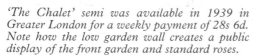

'The Chalet' semi was available in 1939 in Greater London for a weekly payment of 28s 6d. Note how the low garden wall creates a public display of the front garden and standard roses.

CONCLUSION

Despite the availability of modern design, the country cottage look was the most popular interior style of the 1930s. The 'Savoy' range of furnishings illustrated here cost £33 10s from Drages but could be delivered after a deposit of just 15s.

Despite, or perhaps because of, their great popularity, the architectural styles of 1930s housing attracted many critical comments. Suburban estates of semi-detached homes were held in contempt by leading architects and design critics. Even the flat-roofed 'Sun-Trap' villas were criticised for their shallow interpretation of Modern Movement architecture. Such houses were indeed designed simply to appear modern rather than being the product of a modern building process. The acid tongues of critics were sharpest, however, in their attacks on the semi-detached homes in mock-historical styles. This most popular choice for the house-buying public was commonly sneered at as a retrograde step in design. There has long been a conflict of values between those who choose to live in the suburbs and those who work in the professions of architecture and planning, and in the 1930s the opponents of pastiche suburban styles were particularly vocal.

The design critic Anthony Bertram explained the popularity of the 'Tudoresque' as a love based on fear and a wish to escape from the present, from the threat of war and from economic depression. As a functionalist, he could not comprehend why people chose the romantically clad semi-detached home. In 1933 the International

In a department store customers could choose their favourite interior style from completed room-settings. This scrubbed-oak, historically inspired dining-room set cost 39 guineas in 1935.

Congress of Modern Architecture, dominated by the Swiss architect Le Corbusier, attacked the suburbs themselves as a symbol of waste, describing them as 'a kind of scum churning against the walls of the city'.

The continental Modern Movement believed in a future of high-rise living in the city centre, a world away from the sentimental old-world charm of Britain's semi-detached estates. The idealistic

For those looking towards the 'brave new world', the 'Modernity' range was available from Bowmans department store, with an electric fire at £6 10s.

Unfortunately many homes from the period have had replacement windows, destroying the character of the property. This once celebrated Modern villa at Borth in Ceredigion has lost much of its original styling.

'machines for living in' of the Le Corbusier school were innovative and influential, but ultimately they failed to encompass the whims and fancies of the buying public. Although D. H. Lawrence described suburban semis as 'horrid little red mantraps', they were just what the majority of people wanted.

For the generation who first lived in them, 1930s homes were often a new way of seeing and understanding the world. The architectural styles were different, the layout of the houses was new, and the occupants were often experiencing modern technologies and appliances, and the changes that they brought. For many, the new all-electric 1930s home really did represent the 'bright new age'. Owning a suburban semi-detached home or a modernist villa was very different from renting a Victorian terraced house.

Most 1930s British homes were not at the forefront of avant-garde architecture, nor did they fulfil the promise of the rural idyll described in the advertising for suburban estates. The new houses did, however, reflect the dreams of the house-buying population of the time. They proved beyond doubt the importance of romantic notions in the British consciousness and (had architects taken heed) forewarned of the demise of the emerging Internationalist style. Today the high-rise 'machines for living in' from the 1950s and 1960s are being pulled down because few people want to live in them whereas inter-war homes generally retain their value and status in the domestic market. Possibly the 1930s home will always be a pleasant place to live – because it reflects the romance in our nature rather than just our needs.

FURTHER READING

Barrett, Helena, and Phillips, John. *Suburban Style*. Macdonald & Co, 1987.
Gordon, Bob. *Early Electrical Appliances*. Shire, reprinted 1998.
Hill, Jonathan. *Old Radio Sets*. Shire, reprinted 1998.
Jackson, Alan. *Semi-detached London*. Wild Swan, 1991.
Katz, Sylvia. *Early Plastics*. Shire, second edition 1994.
Oliver, Paul, et al. *Dunroamin*. Pimlico, 1981.
Ryan, Deborah. *The Ideal Home through the Twentieth Century*. Hazar, 1997.
Stevenson, Greg. *Art Deco Ceramics*. Shire, 1998.

PLACES TO VISIT

It is always advisable to telephone in advance to check opening arrangements and to find out whether the items that you wish to see are likely to be on display.

Bakelite Museum, Bridge Street, Williton, Taunton, Somerset TA4 4NS. Telephone: 01984 632133. Website: www.bakelitemuseum.co.uk

Carmarthenshire County Museum, Abergwili, Carmarthen SA31 2JG. Telephone: 01267 231691.

Ceredigion Museum, Terrace Road, Aberystwyth, Ceredigion SY23 2AQ. Telephone: 01970 633088. Website: www.ceredigion.gov.uk/coliseum

Croydon Museum, Katharine Street, Croydon CR9 1ET. Telephone: 020 8253 1030.

De La Warr Pavilion, Marina, Bexhill, East Sussex TN40 1DP. Telephone: 01424 787900. Website: www.de-la-warr.pavilion.org.uk

Eltham Palace, Court Yard, off Court Road, London SE9 5QE. Telephone: 020 8294 2548. (English Heritage – website: www.english-heritage.org.uk)

Geffrye Museum, Kingsland Road, London E2 8EA. Telephone: 020 7739 9893. Website: www.geffrye-museum.org.uk

Gnome Reserve, West Putford, Bradworthy, Devon EX22 7XE. Telephone: 01409 241435. Website: www.gnomereserve.co.uk

Museum of Domestic Design and Architecture, Middlesex University, Cat Hill, Barnet, Hertfordshire EN4 8HT. Telephone: 020 8362 5244. Website: www.moda.mdx.ac.uk

Museum of Welsh Life, St Fagans, Cardiff CF5 6XB. Telephone: 029 2057 3500. Website: www.nmgw.ac.uk

Victoria and Albert Museum, Cromwell Road, South Kensington, London SW7 2RL. Telephone: 020 7942 2000. Website: www.vam.ac.uk

2 Willow Road, Hampstead, London NW3 1TH (National Trust). Telephone: 020 7435 6166. One of the few Modernist houses open to the public in Britain, this was the home of the architect Erno Goldfinger, designed and built by him in the 1930s.

Readers may also wish to contact the Twentieth Century Society at 70 Cowcross Street, London EC1M 6EJ (telephone: 020 7250 3857). The makers of the 'Sun-Trap' windows mentioned in the text are Crittall Windows Ltd, Springwood Drive, Braintree, Essex CM7 2YN. Telephone: 01376 324106. Website: www.crittall-windows.co.uk

The lounge at 'Stillness', with French windows leading down to the pool (see also back cover photograph). The house was designed by Gilbert Booth in 1934.